What to Teach When

A Thoughtful and Engaging Music Curriculum

Grades K–1

Brian Hiller
and
Don Dupont

Credits

Editor: Jeanette Morgan
Music Engraver: Linda Taylor
Cover Design and Illustrations: Patti Jeffers
Book Design: WordStreamCopy

Permission-to-Reproduce Notice

Heritage Music Press
A division of The Lorenz Corporation
PO Box 802
Dayton OH 45401
www.lorenz.com

Printed in the United States of America.

ISBN: 978-1-4291-3114-8

HERITAGE MUSIC PRESS

A Lorenz Company • www.lorenz.com

Preface

Teaching is both an art and a science. The art of teaching provides creative, exciting, and enriching activities that engage the learners. The science is the understanding that we (teachers) need to present material in a developmentally appropriate and sequential manner. We want our students to be actively involved in the music-making process and at the same time be able to articulate exactly what they are learning in music. The goal of this series is to provide elementary music specialists with the tools and resources they need to develop a curriculum that teaches skills and concepts while maintaining an aesthetic and creative classroom environment!

The music room is a place where children participate, discover, investigate, learn, and perform. The result is an experience that not only builds musical knowledge but helps students develop a positive attitude toward music. At the elementary levels, students develop skills in music through singing, chanting, moving, and playing instruments. In our classrooms, we often integrate all of the music-making activities into one learning experience. For example, children may learn a traditional folk song, identify the form and style, add movement and instrumental accompaniment, and develop ideas for contrasting sections. This multifaceted approach fosters active music participation and allows individual students an opportunity to express themselves. Through this process the children learn to become not only independent musicians but interdependent members of a community of learners.

Every elementary student in our district attends music once a week. As in any other discipline, music has its own tools, materials, concepts, and skills, which are developed with increasing understanding over time. For each concept or skill, the student must pass through a learning sequence to assimilate and build understanding.

What to Teach When: A Thoughtful and Engaging Music Curriculum Grades K–1 provides elementary music specialists with repertoire and learning activities for teaching the elements of rhythm, melody, form, texture, and timbre. The curriculum is spiraled and the order of the activities has been carefully designed so that skills and concepts are continually reinforced before new concepts are introduced. Each song or activity lists the elemental focus and concept along with the basic way in which we teach the piece to our students. When applicable, you will see thumbnail images of the visual aids and/or manipulatives we have created for teaching the piece. All of these can be found on the CD-ROM included with this book and they may be projected to a screen or whiteboard, or printed to make a more traditional poster-type visual.

Our goal is to provide you with the repertoire which will form the core of your curriculum. We encourage you to use the ideas in this publication as a springboard to creating exciting and enriching experiences with your students. At the end of each grade-level offering, you will find samples of fully processed lesson plans that demonstrate how particular music skills and concepts might be taught in more detail. We wish you all the best!

Brian Hiller   Don Dupont

Kindergarten

Kindergarten is such a milestone! Students are learning so much, and it is crucial to set the stage for your expectations, classroom procedures, and joyful music exploration and creation. In our classes, kindergarten students participate in a variety of singing games, movement activities, and dances to develop a feeling of steady beat. Students also learn to differentiate between speaking and singing voices and begin to develop the ability to sing in tune. The students explore simple forms, learn to differentiate between monophonic and polyphonic music, and learn about the common timbres of classroom instruments.

Specific goals for each element are listed below and referenced in the repertoire on the following pages.

Rhythm

- Maintain a steady beat
- Identify silent beats
- Identify tempo (slow/slower; fast/faster)
- Move to various meters ($\frac{2}{4}$, $\frac{3}{4}$, $\frac{4}{4}$, $\frac{6}{8}$)
- Perform durations longer and shorter than the beat

Melody

- Differentiate between speaking and singing voices
- Explore expressive vocal qualities
- Explore high and low
- Develop a sense of melodic contour
- Foster in-tune singing (one, two, and three pitches)

Form

- Identify phrases through chanting, singing, moving, and instrument playing
- Perform call-and-response
- Identify verse and refrain
- Learn cumulative songs
- Learn counting songs

Texture

- Distinguish between monophonic and polyphonic music
- Perform the beat while chanting and singing

Timbre

- Explore vocal qualities (singing, speaking, whispering, and shouting)
- Perform body percussion (snap, clap, pat, and stamp)
- Identify non-pitched percussion instruments by sound and family (woods, metals, skins)

Setting the Stage with Bubble Space

We begin the year in kindergarten by introducing the students to "bubble space." This teaching tool is a verbal cue and direction we use throughout the year to encourage safe and responsible movement throughout the music room. Before we begin a movement activity, we instruct students to begin and end in the same bubble space. As they move about the room, they must take care not to let their bubbles pop!

Have your students create their own bubble space by finding a place in the room where they can slowly turn with outstretched arms without touching anyone or anything. Then, have the students blow imaginary bubbles around themselves. Explain that they must take care when moving around the room to keep their bubbles from popping (they don't want to get too close to anyone or anything).

Practice having students move to their bubble spaces; move freely throughout the room; and then return to the places they started in by the end of the song or music.

Bubble space is also referred to as self-space or personal space.

Rhythm: Move to various meters ($\frac{2}{4}$, $\frac{3}{4}$, $\frac{4}{4}$, $\frac{6}{8}$)

I Can Walk

Hiller/Dupont

I can *walk* and *walk,* I can *walk* and *walk,* I can *walk* a-round the town!

Sing the song and move about the room to the steady beat. Change the words and movement to correspond to changes in meter. For example: march to $\frac{4}{4}$ meter, gallop to $\frac{6}{8}$, and slide to $\frac{3}{4}$.

Singing with Mr. Bear

Throughout our lessons, we model and reinforce in-tune singing, usually staying within the keys of C or D for young voices. Typically, the only reason a student sings out of tune is because we allow him or her to do so! At the beginning of the year, we introduce Mr. Bear, a teddy-bear hand puppet. Students echo motives on "loo" in the following sequence: *sol–mi, sol–sol–mi, sol–la–sol, sol–la–sol–mi.* The puppet does a little dance when the students sing in tune.

Melody: Differentiate between speaking and singing voices

Baa, Baa, Black Sheep

Traditional
Arr. Hiller/Dupont

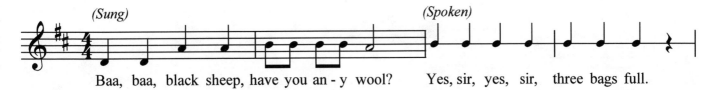

Baa, baa, black sheep, have you an-y wool? Yes, sir, yes, sir, three bags full.

One for my mas-ter, one for my dame, one for the lit-tle boy who lives down the lane.

Baa, baa, black sheep, have you an-y wool? Yes, sir, yes, sir, three bags full.

Perform the song for your students, alternating between a singing voice and a speaking voice as indicated. Have the students raise their hands when they hear the singing.

Timbre: Explore vocal qualities (singing, speaking, whispering, and shouting)

Listen as I Whisper

Hiller/Dupont

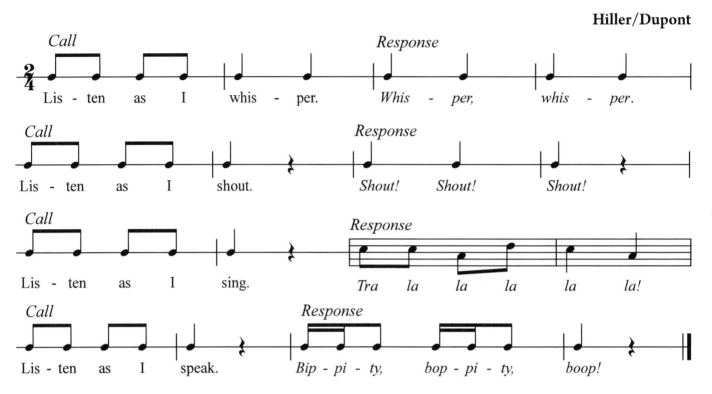

1. Perform the chant for your students. Teach the students each response.
2. Next, speak the call and have the students speak the responses using the voice quality indicated in the text.
3. Invite four students to stand in front of the class, one for each response. Have the class speak the calls and have each student perform his or her response. We use four puppets, Whisper, Shout, Sing, and Speak, to reinforce the idea of different vocal qualities. During the performance, each soloist can have his or her puppet mime the response along with the soloist.

"Listen as I Whisper" is from *Make a Joyful Sound* (Dupont/Hiller), © 2007 Memphis Musicraft Publications. Used by permission.

Clap the Beat

Traditional
Arr. Hiller/Dupont

1. Have your students stand in a circle with a leader in the center. (For the first experience, you should be the leader, followed by confident students.)
2. During the song, the leader maintains a steady beat using body percussion (clap, snap, pat, stamp) as the rest of the class imitates simultaneously. Change the words accordingly (*snap* the beat, *pat* the beat, *stamp* the beat) and repeat the song several times with new leaders.

Rhythm: Maintain a steady beat (non-pitched percussion)

Johnny Works with One Hammer

Traditional

1. Have your students stand in self-space and sing the song while keeping the steady beat as follows: one hammer = one fist on one thigh; two hammers = two fists on two thighs; three hammers = add left foot; four hammers = add right foot; five hammers = nod head.
2. Set up five chairs and direct five students to sit on them. Give each of the children on the chairs a non-pitched percussion instrument. Sing the song, substituting each child's name in turn as he or she plays the steady beat on his or her instrument (for example: Mary works with one hammer, Billy works with two hammers). Make the game additive so that at the end, all five students are playing.

The Grand Old Duke of York

Traditional
Arr. Hiller/Dupont

The grand old duke of York, he had ten thou-sand men. He *(Spoken)*

marched them up to the top of the hill and he marched them down a-gain. And

when they were up, they were up. And when they were down, they were down. And

when they were on-ly half-way up, they were nei-ther up nor down!

1. As a warm-up, use rides at an amusement park as a fun way to experiment with sounds that move up or down or stay at one level. Have the children provide sound effects for a roller coaster, a water slide, and a Ferris wheel and move their arms to accompany the sounds.
2. Sing "The Grand Old Duke of York" while marching higher and lower as indicated by the text. Speak with high and low voices to match the text in the spoken section.
3. Have the students accompany the speaking part on barred instruments, playing on the high, low, and middle parts of the instruments as indicated by the text.

Here I Come

Hiller/Dupont

Here I come with my big bass drum.   Hear me play with a rum-tum-tum!

Here I come with my bells that ring.   Hear me play with a ring-ting-ting!

1. Have the students speak the chant using low and high voices.
2. Next, have them march around the room to the beat of a drum.
3. Choose students to play drums on "rum-tum-tum" and bells or triangles on "ring-ting-ting." Rotate on repetitions of the song.

Form: Identify phrases through chanting, singing, moving, and instrument playing

Cobbler, Cobbler

Traditional
Arr. Hiller/Dupont

Woodblocks   *Triangles*

Cob - bler, Cob - bler, mend my shoe.   Get it done by half past two.

Sandblocks   *Hand drums*

Stitch it up, stitch it down,   then I'll give you half a crown.

1. Teach the chant phrase by phrase until it is secure. Have the students speak the chant while patting a steady beat on their legs. At the beginning of each phrase, play a triangle one time to indicate a new phrase is beginning and to mark the length of the phrases.
2. Next, have the students stand in self-space and walk to the beat as they chant the rhyme, changing direction at the beginning of each phrase (cue them with the triangle).
3. Transfer the rhythm of the chant to non-pitched percussion as indicated in the score. Speak and play at the same time, then play only.

Wee Willie Winkie

Traditional

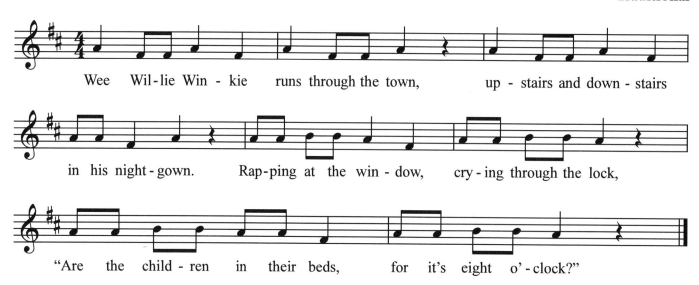

1. Sing the song, drawing an arch on the board for each phrase. Sing the song again and "draw" an arch in the air for each phrase as your students simultaneously imitate the movement.

2. Teach the following motions:

Lyrics	Movements
Wee Willie Winkie runs through the town,	Move arms to the beat as if walking.
Upstairs and downstairs in his nightgown.	Sway side to side.
Rapping at the window, crying through the lock,	Imitate knocking on a door.
"Are the children in their beds, for it's eight o'clock?"	Point to wrist as if looking at a watch.

3. Teach and play the following game: Have the students stand in self-space and tell them that they are in their houses and have to stay in them until Willie visits. Assign one child to be Willie. Explain how as the class sings the song, Willie will walk around the room. On "Rapping at the window," he or she will stop in front of a student and perform the movement. Then he/she will trade places with the student who was standing and sit down on the floor in his or her "house" to pantomime sleeping. The new student will assume the role of Willie. Continue in this manner until all students have had a turn to be Willie (and are seated). The last child to be selected should play the role of Town Crier, tip-toeing through the classroom to make sure that all students are "asleep."

Engine, Engine Number Nine

Traditional

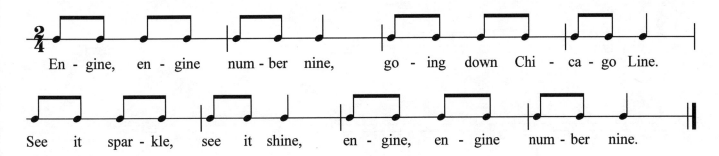

En - gine, en - gine num - ber nine, go - ing down Chi - ca - go Line.

See it spar - kle, see it shine, en - gine, en - gine num - ber nine.

This song introduces an iconic representation of the steady beat.

1. Display the Steady Beat Visual. Speak the chant, pointing to each engine/beat with a mallet as the students pat the beat on their legs.
2. Next, have student "conductors" take turns pointing to the beats as the class speaks the chant.

This visual aid is available as a digital file on the accompanying CD. You can project this page to a screen or whiteboard or print it to make a more traditional poster-type visual.

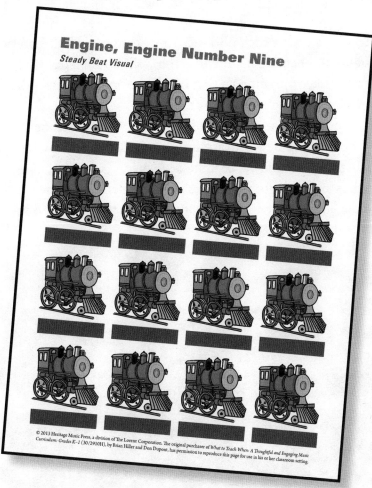

Charlie Over the Ocean

Traditional

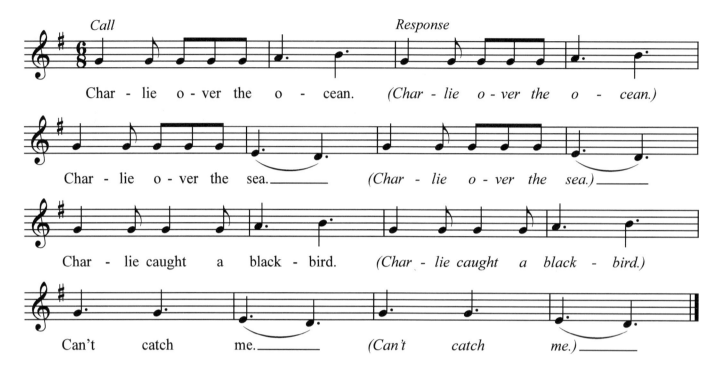

Char - lie o - ver the o - cean. (Char - lie o - ver the o - cean.)

Char - lie o - ver the sea._____ (Char - lie o - ver the sea.)_____

Char - lie caught a black - bird. (Char - lie caught a black - bird.)

Can't catch me._____ (Can't catch me.)_____

1. Sing the song phrase by phrase. After each phrase is sung, echo the phrase on the recorder or piano. Ask the students to describe what is happening. Identify the "call" and "response."

2. Sing the song as written and have the students provide the response. Invite individual students to perform the call and supply simple motions to accompany the text.

3. Teach and play the following game: Students stand in a circle with one student (the caller) on the outside. As the caller leads the song, she or he walks around the circle, tapping each student on the shoulder. At the end of the song, the caller takes the hand of the last person tapped. The pair skips around the outside of the circle while the class keeps the beat and you play the melody on the piano or another instrument. When they get back to the empty spot, the current caller joins the circle and the game continues with the last person who was tapped as the new caller.

Sing Your Name

Hiller/Dupont

Sing the song and have students sing their names using a *sol-mi* motive. The class should echo the child's name. After four students have had a turn, sing the song again. Continue in this manner until all have had a turn.

Walking, Walking

Hiller/Dupont

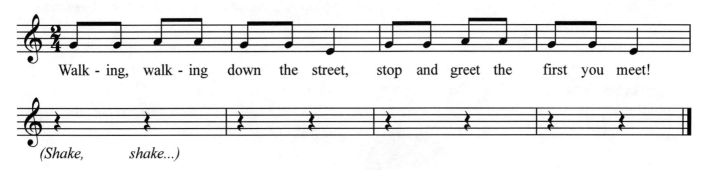

1. Play the game Red Light, Green Light as follows: Students stand in self-space. When you say, "Green light!" the students move out of their self-space and walk to the beat of a drum that you play. When you say, "Red light!" the students stop and bounce in place to the beat, waiting for the light to "change."
2. Teach "Walking, Walking" by rote. Introduce the following movement to accompany the song: Students sing the song and walk to the steady beat. On the words "first you meet," each student stops in front of a partner and shakes hands to the silent beat. The game continues with new partners. Display the Steady Beat Visual. Sing the song, pointing to the beats/shoes. Have the students determine where the silent beats occur. Cover the silent beats with construction paper or sticky notes. Sing the song, with the children patting their legs for the beats with sound and lightly tapping their chests for the silent beats.
3. Explore other combinations of beat/silent beat placement using the visual.

This visual aid is available as a digital file on the accompanying CD.

● ● ● **Kindergarten** ● ● ●   15

Time for Instruments

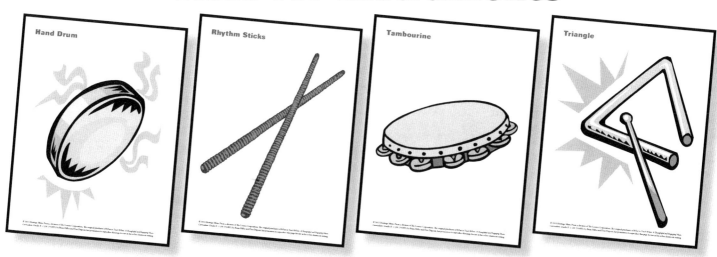

1. Present the Instrument Visual Aids (available on the CD).
2. Divide the class into four groups, giving one group drums, the next group triangles, the next group rhythm sticks, and the final group tambourines.
3. Play a piece of music, and as you point to one of the visual aids, have the group assigned to that instrument maintain a steady beat.
4. Have each group play in turn (monophonic) and then have combinations of instruments play (polyphonic).
5. Play this listening game: Have one student from each group take his or her instrument and stand behind a blackboard or piano, out of view. Without letting the class know whom you're choosing, direct one or two of the musicians to play the steady beat. Have the rest of the class identify the instruments that are playing.

Hurry, Little Pony

Spanish Folk Song
Arr. Hiller/Dupont

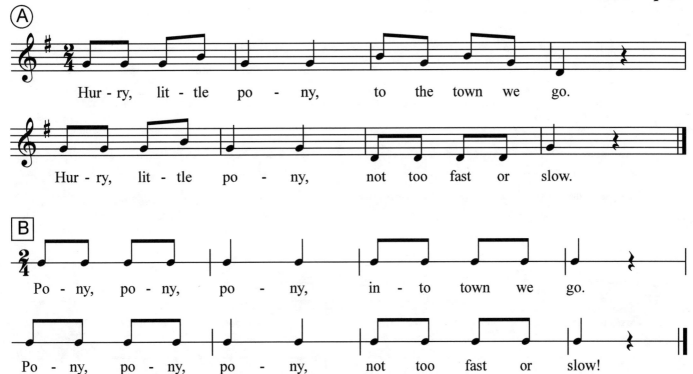

Ⓐ

Hur - ry,   lit - tle   po - ny,   to   the   town   we   go.

Hur - ry,   lit - tle   po - ny,   not   too   fast   or   slow.

Ⓑ

Po - ny,   po - ny,   po - ny,   in - to   town   we   go.

Po - ny,   po - ny,   po - ny,   not   too   fast   or   slow!

Students need many experiences with maintaining a steady beat before they are ready to perform both the beat and the rhythm simultaneously.

1. Teach the song by rote.
2. Once the students are familiar with the song, have them stand in a circle with one student in the center. If you have a hobbyhorse, allow the student in the center to hold it. After singing the A section, the students should chant the B section while maintaining a steady beat on their legs. The student in the middle should gallop inside the circle. During the repeat of the song, choose a new student to go into the center.

This Is the Way the Ladies Ride

Traditional
Arr. Hiller/Dupont

V — This is the way the la - dies ride: trit, trot, trit, trot.

BP — *(snap)*

V — This is the way the gen - tle - men ride: jig - ge - ty jog, jig - ge - ty jog.

BP — *(clap)*

V — This is the way the farm - ers ride: hob - ble - ty hoy, hob - ble - ty hoy.

BP — *(pat)*

V — This is the way the hunt - ers ride: gal - lo - py, gal - lo - py o - ver the fence!

BP — *(stamp)*

1. Speak the poem for your students, modeling the body percussion.
2. Once the class is familiar with the chant and the body percussion, allow individual students to lead the class with the body percussion of their choosing.

Form: Identify verse and refrain

Rig-a-Jig-Jig

Traditional

Verse

As I was walk-ing down the street, down the street, down the street, a

spe-cial per-son I did meet, heigh-ho, heigh-ho, heigh-ho!

Refrain

Rig-a-jig-jig and a-way we go, a-way we go, a-way we go.

Rig-a-jig-jig and a-way we go, heigh-ho, heigh-ho, heigh-ho.

1. Sing the song and ask your students to raise their hands when they hear the part of the song with the nonsense word (*rig-a-jig-jig*). Identify the verse and the refrain.
2. Teach the following movements:
   Formation: Students stand in self-space.
   Verse: Students walk around the room to the beat of the song.
   Refrain: Each student joins hands with a partner, turning in place.

● ● ● **Kindergarten** ● ● ●

Hickory, Dickory, Dock

Traditional
Arr. Hiller/Dupont

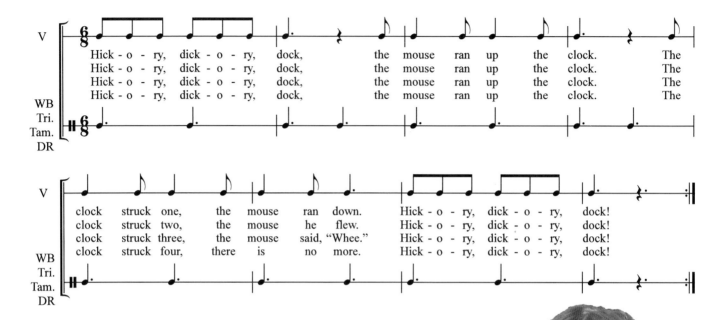

1. Divide the class into four groups. Distribute woodblocks, triangles, drums, and tambourines, assigning one instrument type to each group.
2. Have each group maintain the steady beat on the instruments for their verse, when it is spoken.
3. Have the children think of combinations of instruments to play simultaneously to add to the texture.

Sing, Dance, Chant, and Play

Hiller/Dupont

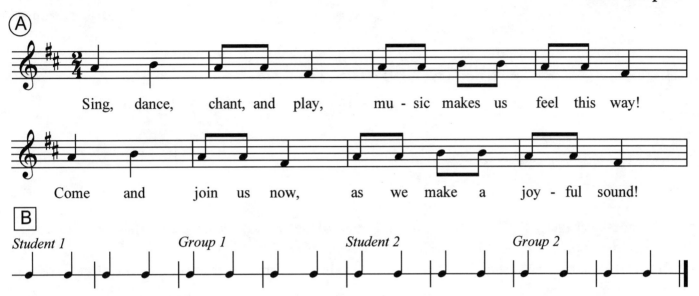

1. With students in self-space, distribute drums, tambourines, rhythm sticks, and triangles.
2. Identify each instrument's family (skins, metals, woods).
3. Have four students stand in front of the class, each with a different instrument. Sing the song. On the B section, have one student play four beats. Students with that instrument echo. Then, have the second student play four beats and students with that instrument echo. Continue in this manner with the remaining instruments.

Move to the Tempo

Use this activity to explore various tempi with your students: With students in self-space, each holding a pair of rhythm sticks, play a song on the piano. Invite students to tap the beat by clicking their sticks together. When the music stops, have the students tap their sticks on the floor for eight beats at the same tempo as the song. Continue the game by playing songs that are faster and slower.

Higglety, Pigglety, Pop!

Traditional Text
Arr. Hiller/Dupont

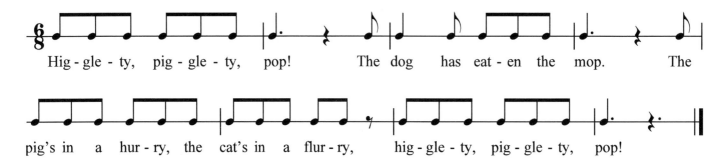

Hig - gle - ty, pig - gle - ty, pop! The dog has eat - en the mop. The

pig's in a hur - ry, the cat's in a flur - ry, hig - gle - ty, pig - gle - ty, pop!

1. Present the Higglety, Pigglety, Pop! Visual Aid and read the poem (as notated above) for your students.
2. Teach the chant by having students echo you phrase by phrase.
3. Once the class is familiar with the chant, lead the students in patting a steady beat on their legs. Speak the poem at this tempo.
4. Next, increase the tempo and speak the poem faster. Continue in this manner with faster (and slower) tempi.

Drip, Drip, Drip

Hiller/Dupont

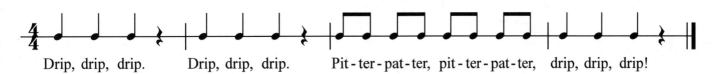

Drip, drip, drip.   Drip, drip, drip.   Pit-ter-pat-ter, pit-ter-pat-ter, drip, drip, drip!

1. Have your students listen to you speak "Drip, Drip, Drip" while maintaining the steady beat on a drum. Have the students identify where sounds are shorter than the beat.
2. Teach the chant by rote.
3. In bubble space, invite the students to move to reflect the rhythms.
4. Transfer the rhythms to two contrasting non-pitched percussion instruments.

Hammer Ring

American Folk Song

Don't you   hear   the   ham-mer   ring-ing,   ham-mer   ring,   ham-mer   ring?

Don't you   hear   the   ham-mer   ring-ing,   ham-mer   ring,   ham-mer   ring?

1. Have your students listen to you sing "Hammer Ring" and identify where sounds are longer than the beat.
2. Sing the song again, patting the quarter notes and clapping the half notes. (Show the duration of the half notes by raising the top hand higher on the clap.)
3. Decide which instruments would best represent the two sounds and have the class perform the song, integrating the instruments.

One, Two, Tie My Shoe

Traditional

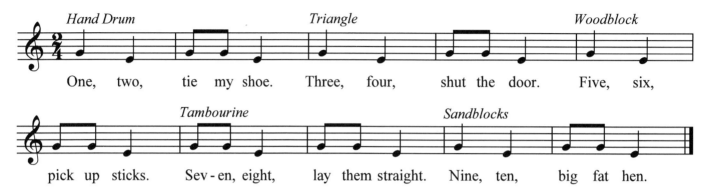

One, two, tie my shoe. Three, four, shut the door. Five, six,

pick up sticks. Sev-en, eight, lay them straight. Nine, ten, big fat hen.

1. Teach the song, echoing by phrases.
2. Once the class is familiar with it, sing the song as the students clap on the number words.
3. Place the non-pitched percussion instruments in a row in the order indicated in the score. Assign equal groups of students to sit in a line behind each of the instruments.
4. As the class sings the song, each student at the front of the line plays his or her instrument on the number words in order. When the song is over, the students who played go to the back of their lines.
5. Sing the song again with new players. For an added challenge, internalize all the number words.

Rhythm: Recognize duration (shorter and longer than the beat)

Hot Cross Buns

Traditional

Hot cross buns, hot cross buns. One a pen-ny, two a pen-ny, hot cross buns.

Sing "Hot Cross Buns" and transfer the rhythms to non-pitched percussion as follows: quarter notes on hand drums, half notes on triangles, and eighth notes on woodblocks.

Bought Me a Cat

Traditional

Bought me a cat,   cat   pleased   me.   Fed   my
Bought me a hen,   hen   pleased   me.   Fed   my

1.

cat   by   yon - der   tree.   Cat   goes,   "Fid-dle - i - fee."
hen   by   yon - der   tree.

2.

Hen   goes,   "Chip - sy,   chop - sy,"   cat   goes,   "Fid - dle - i - fee."

1. Sing the song for your students in cumulative fashion adding a new verse each time the song is repeated, and always ending with "Cat goes, 'Fiddle-i-fee.'"
2. Display the "Bought Me a Cat" Visual Aid, and invite your students to join you in singing the animal sounds.
3. Once students are familiar with the song, divide the class into groups, assigning each group to an animal. Distribute instruments to the groups.
4. Have the students accompany the text with instruments as indicated below:

Bought Me a Cat
Visual Aid

Cat goes, "Fiddle-i-fee."
Hen goes, "Chipsy, chopsy."
Duck goes, "Quack, quack."
Goose goes, "Swishy, swashy."
Dog goes, "Bowwow, bowwow."
Sheep goes, "Baa, baa."
Pig goes, "Griffy, gruffy."
Goat goes, "Bleat, bleat."
Cow goes, "Moo, moo."

Lyrics	Instruments
Cat goes, "Fiddle-i-fee."	Play A–G–F on alto xylophones.
Hen goes, "Chipsy, chopsy."	Play A–C, A–C on glockenspiels.
Duck goes, "Quack, quack."	Play on guiros.
Goose goes, "Swishy, swashy."	Play on sandblocks.
Dog goes, "Bowwow, bowwow."	Play on woodblocks.
Sheep goes, "Baa, baa."	Play on finger cymbals.
Pig goes, "Griffy, gruffy."	Play on cabasas.
Goat goes, "Bleat, bleat."	Play on tambourines.
Cow goes, "Moo, moo."	Play on large drums with mallets.

Sample Lesson Plan

Kindergarten

Focus: Develop a sense of melodic contour
Skills: Maintain a steady beat • Explore high and low • Play instruments

Engine, Engine Number Nine

Traditional
Arr. Hiller/Dupont

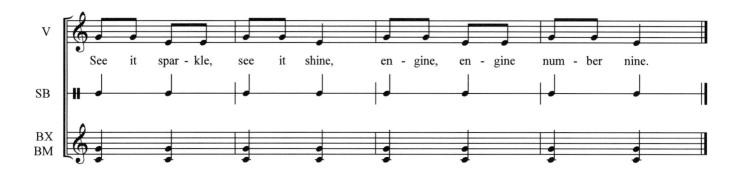

Process

1. With your students in self-space, explore ways of moving high and low. Play high and low sounds on the piano to guide the movement.
2. Next, use a hand puppet to guide students in singing the echo patterns below. When the students sing in tune, the puppet should do a little dance!

3. Repeat the activity using body levels for students to echo (*sol* = hands on shoulders, *mi* = hands on waist).
4. Teach "Engine, Engine Number Nine" by echoing phrases (by rote). Reinforce the melodic contour by using the body levels described previously as you sing.

26   ● ● ● **Kindergarten** ● ● ●

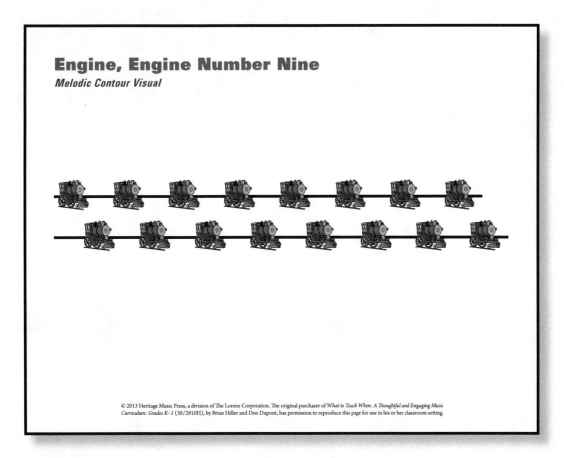

Engine, Engine Number Nine
Melodic Contour Visual

5. Present the Melodic Contour Visual.

6. Sing "Engine, Engine Number Nine" to the class. While you sing, point to the train icons (quarter-note pulse) outlining the melodic contour (start with the higher line of trains on the *sol* line and then move to the lower line of trains to show *mi*). Invite student leaders to be the "conductor."

7. Prepare the orchestration using body percussion. Transfer to instruments.

8. Introduce the game Get on Board: Have the students stand in self-space. Choose a leader to be the "engine." As the class sings the song, the leader walks about the room, moving her or his arms like the wheels of a train. At the end of the song, the leader stands behind another student, who becomes the new engine. The "train" is now two "cars" long! Continue in this manner until all have had a turn as leader.

Extensions

To create a contrasting section, transfer the steady-beat accompaniment to barred instruments set up in C-pentatonic (remove F and B bars). Instruct the students to play clusters (any two notes) in a pattern beginning with the high (short) bars and then the low (long) bars (high, low, high, low, etc.).

If you wish, print, copy, and distribute the Kindergarten Assessment found on the CD and page 28.

Name: _____ Classroom Teacher: _____ Date: _____

Kindergarten Assessment
Melodic Contour

Circle what you hear!

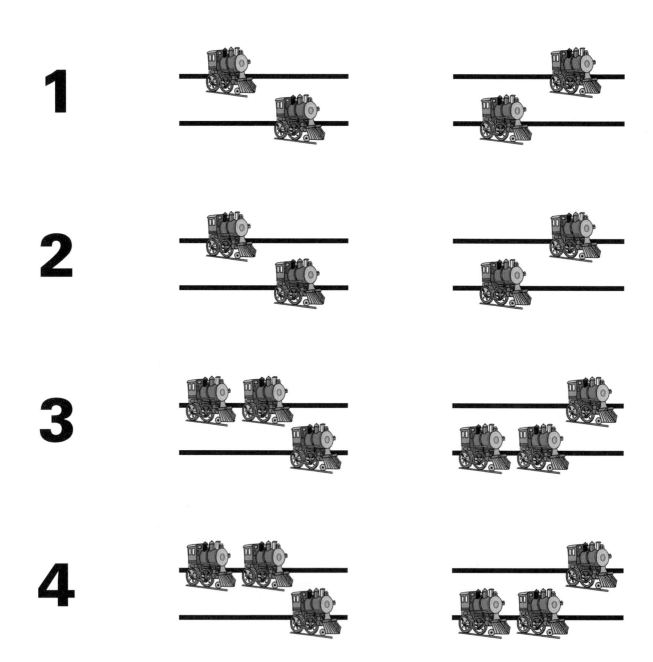

Instructions for the teacher: Sing one of the motives from each example using the syllable "loo." Use body levels if desired. Have the students sing it back with or without the body levels and then circle what they hear.

First Grade

In first grade, students begin linking words and music. Beginning experiences with text are aided by repetition, rhyme, rhythm, pattern, and predictability. Students learn to differentiate between the steady beat and the rhythm. The rhythms of a quarter note and two eighth notes are introduced, along with the quarter rest. Students manipulate these rhythms with a variety of poems, nursery rhymes, and story songs. They transfer rhythms to percussion instruments and begin to experience improvisation.

First-grade students can match pitches with hand signs, which aids in pitch recognition and in-tune singing. First graders are also able to identify binary form and hold their parts when playing simple accompaniments and *ostinati*.

The specific goals for each element are listed below and in the repertoire on the following pages.

Rhythm

- Explore quarter notes, eighth notes, and quarter rests through movement
- Experience quarter notes
- Identify quarter notes
- Identify quarter rest
- Experience eighth notes
- Identify eighth notes
- Differentiate between rhythm and beat
- Notate quarter notes, two eighth notes, and quarter rests

Melody

- Listen for upward, downward, and repeated pitches
- Sing, play, and identify *sol* and *mi* (or *sol*, *la*, and *mi*)
- Identify phrases in chants and songs

Form

- Identify phrases in chants and songs
- Identify phrases that are the same and that are different
- Recognize A (repeated form)
- Recognize AB (binary form)

Texture

- Perform rhythm patterns over the beat
- Perform simple accompaniments on barred instruments
- Perform simple ostinati to accompany text

Timbre

- Identify and play a variety of non-pitched percussion instruments
- Transfer text rhythms to body percussion and non-pitched percussion
- Explore the sound qualities of the barred instruments

I'm Gonna Build

Folk Song
Arr. Hiller/Dupont

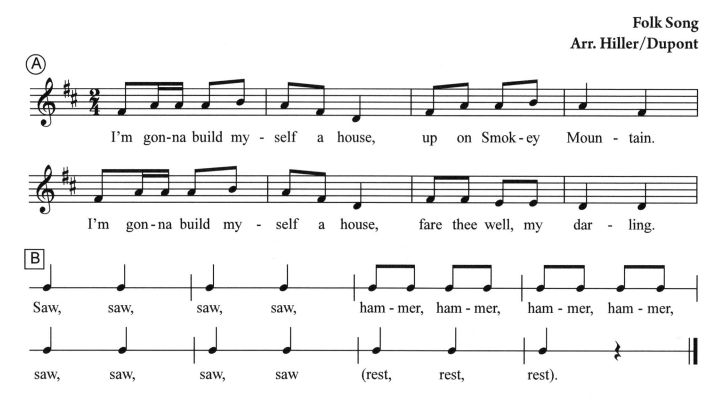

Ⓐ

I'm gon-na build my - self a house, up on Smok-ey Moun - tain.

I'm gon-na build my - self a house, fare thee well, my dar - ling.

B

Saw, saw, saw, saw, ham - mer, ham - mer, ham - mer, ham - mer,

saw, saw, saw, saw (rest, rest, rest).

1. Divide the class into two groups (saws and hammers). Create movements to accompany the B section.
2. Next, distribute hand drums for the saws and woodblocks for the hammers. Present the Visual Aid:

3. Sing the song and have the students play their instruments on the B section as indicated on the visual.

"I'm Gonna Build" is from *Make a Joyful Sound* (Dupont/Hiller), © 2007 Memphis Musicraft Publications. Used by permission.

Rhythm Band

Distribute triangles, drums, tambourines, and shakers. Present the Rhythm Band Visual. Play a lively piece of music, such as a Sousa march. Point to each beat with a mallet or stick and have the students play along as indicated on the chart.

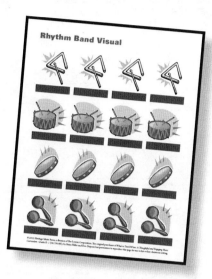

Feel the Phrase

Explain how a musical phrase is a short musical thought usually lasting four to eight beats in length. The end of a phrase can be thought of as a natural breathing point in music.

While maintaining a steady beat on a drum, have the children move their bodies, changing their movements every four beats as you say: "Push, pull, press, stretch, curl, twist, dig." Gradually increase to eight-beat phrases.

The Eensy-Weensy Spider

Traditional

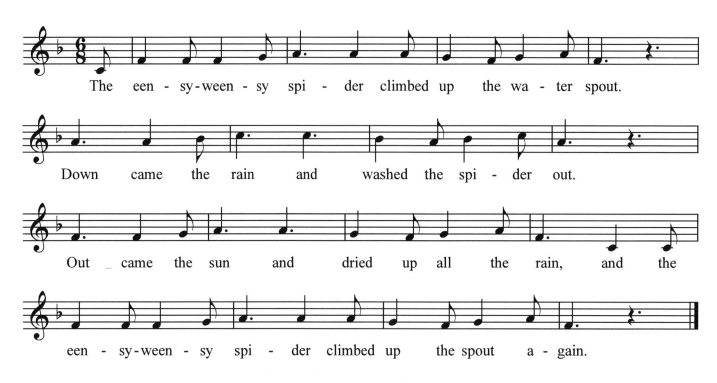

The een - sy-ween - sy spi - der climbed up the wa - ter spout.

Down came the rain and washed the spi - der out.

Out _ came the sun and dried up all the rain, and the

een - sy-ween - sy spi - der climbed up the spout a - gain.

1. Sing the song and create motions or movements to illustrate each phrase.
2. Listen to "*Ah, vous dirai-je, Maman,*" K. 265 ("Twinkle, Twinkle, Little Star"), by Mozart. Experiment with different ways of moving to indicate each phrase.

Little Birdie in the Tree

Hiller/Dupont

Lit - tle bird - ie in the tree, will you sing a song for me?

Lit - tle bird - ie in the tree, sing it sweet as it can be.

1. Discuss with your students ways in which we are the same (two eyes, two ears, etc.) and different (our names, our likes and dislikes, etc.). Explain that in music, parts can be the same and different as well.

2. Speak "Little Birdie in the Tree," maintaining a steady-beat pulse by patting your legs. Point out the phrases that have the same text.

3. Divide the class in half and assign the phrases that have the same text to one group and the phrases that are different to the other. Speak the chant again with each group speaking its part. Students can add motions to further demonstrate same and different.

Little Bo-Peep

Traditional
Arr. Hiller/Dupont

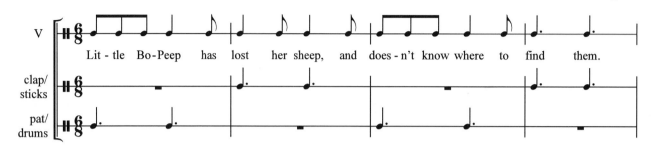

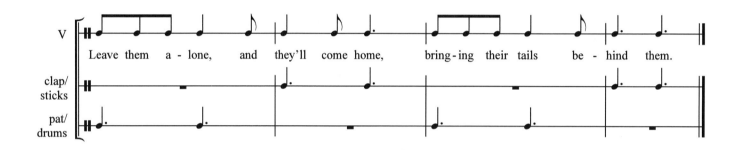

1. Have the students pat a steady beat on their legs while chanting the rhyme.
2. Next, perform the beat using body percussion as indicated in the score.
3. Transfer the body percussion to non-pitched percussion as indicated.
4. Place two drums and two pair of sticks in a row with students in lines behind them. Have the students take turns maintaining the steady-beat pattern. During the interlude, students who played should go to the back of their lines and the next students should play the accompaniment on the repeat.

Little Mousie

Hiller/Dupont

Lit - tle   Mous - ie,   Lit - tle   Mous - ie   lives in - side her   lit - tle   hous - ie!

1. Display the Visual Aid.
2. Speak "Little Mousie" as you point to each beat.
3. Speak the chant again and draw a vertical line on each beat bar to represent one sound per beat (*ta*).
4. Next, play the rhythm of the chant on percussion instruments, one line per instrument group.

'Round and 'Round

Hiller/Dupont

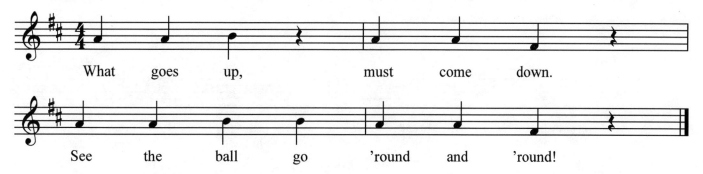

What   goes   up,   must   come   down.

See   the   ball   go   'round   and   'round!

1. Sing "'Round and 'Round," pointing to the Steady Beat Visual. Have the students identify beats where no sound occurs. Sing the song again, drawing the quarter-note and quarter-rest symbols on the beat bars.
2. Play this circle game: With students seated in a circle with four non-pitched percussion instruments in the center, sing the song, passing a ball on every beat. The student who has the ball on the final "round" chooses three classmates to join him or her in the center of the circle to play the rhythm of the song on the instruments. The students return to the circle and the game continues.

"'Round and 'Round" is from *It's Elemental 2: More Lessons That Engage* (Dupont/Hiller), © 2004 Memphis Musicraft Publications. Used by permission.

Melody: Listen for upward, downward, and repeated pitches

Bow, Wow, Wow

Traditional

1. Sing the song using body levels: begin by crouching down, and raise up or down according to the melodic contour of the song.
2. Play the melody on a recorder as your students repeat the activity, internalizing the text.
3. Identify the upward, downward, and repeated tones.

Melody: Sing, play, and identify sol *and* mi

What Did You Have for Breakfast?

Hiller

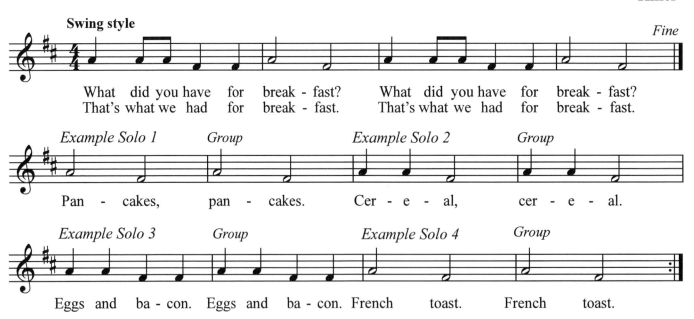

1. Choose four students to answer your question.
2. Sing the song and have the four students sing what they ate for breakfast, placing their hands on their shoulders for the high note (*sol*) and on their waists for the lower note (*mi*). The class should echo as indicated in the score.

Brown Bear, Brown Bear

Adapted from the book by Bill Martin Jr.
Arr. Hiller/Dupont

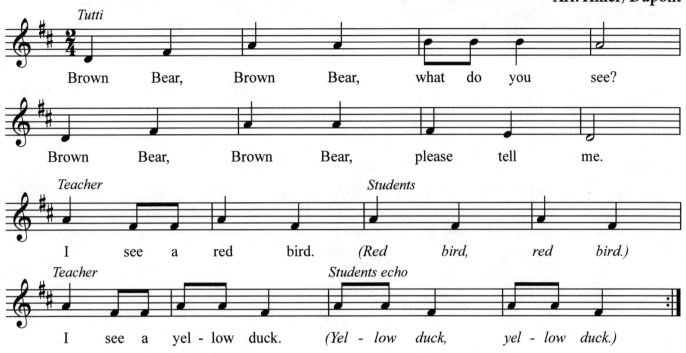

1. Choose a few animals featured in *Brown Bear, Brown Bear, What Do You See?* by Bill Martin Jr, and sing the phrases (red bird, yellow duck, etc) using *sol-mi* patterns and hand signs, instructing the students to echo you.
2. Teach measures 1–8.
3. Sing measures 1–8 as an introduction to the story. Then, show the students the book, and using the illustrations as a guide (not the text of the book), perform the story with your class by singing an "I see" phrase for each animal illustrated and then have the students echo that animal. Measures 9–16 in the score above outline this process. After you have looked at and sung the phrase for two animal illustrations, sing measures 1–8 again. Continue in this manner, singing measures 1–8 after every two animals. At the end of the story, indicate for the students not to sing and then change the lyrics of measure 1–8 to "Children, children…." Point to each animal illustrated and have the students sing the color and animal.

Drum's Birthday

Hiller/Dupont

1. Divide the students into small groups and distribute the percussion instruments named in the chant.
2. Modeling good technique, demonstrate how to play each instrument.
3. Speak the text and then invite the group named to play the rhythm indicated.
4. Once the class is familiar with the chant, invite five individual students to each speak one of the vocal lines and have the students with that instrument respond. Have the entire class sing and play the final four measures.

Skip to My Lou

Traditional

Flies in the but-ter-milk, shoo, fly, shoo. Flies in the but-ter-milk, shoo, fly, shoo.

Flies in the but-ter-milk, shoo, fly, shoo. Skip to my lou, my dar - ling!

2. Little red wagon, painted blue. …
3. Lost my partner, what'll I do? …
4. I'll find another one, just like you. …

1. Sing verse 1 for the students and have them tell you which phrase is different from the others. Teach the song by rote.
2. With the students in pairs, teach the following motions:
    Measure 1: Wiggle fingers to imitate buzzing flies.
    Measure 2: Shake out hands three times ("shoo, fly, shoo").
    Measures 3–4, 5–6: Repeat measures 1–2.
    Measures 7–8: Hold arms in front and turn around each other.
3. Divide the class into four groups, one group for each verse. Direct each group to create the movements for its verse, making sure that the movement for the first three phrases is the same. Note: The students who are responsible for the movements for Verse 1 may choose to use the movements the class learned together or make up new movements.

Student Rhythms

1. In self-space, have students respond to the sound of a drum as follows: for quarter notes, students should walk the beat, saying, "Walk"; for eighth notes, students should pair up and with arms around shoulders, step eighth notes, saying, "Jogging."
2. Set up four chairs representing four beats. Explain how one student per chair equals a quarter note (*ta*); two students per chair equals a pair of eighth notes (*ti-ti*); no student equals a rest. Select and arrange students in the chairs in various rhythm patterns. Have the class speak and then clap each "rhythm."

Rhythm: Identify eighth notes

Seesaw

Traditional

See - saw,   up   and down,   in   the   air and   on   the ground.

1. Teach the song, echoing by phrases.
2. Have the students, in pairs holding hands, face each other and move up and down to the beat as if riding a seesaw.
3. Present the Beat Bar Visual. Sing the song, pointing to each beat. Have students identify where two sounds on the beat occur (*ti-ti*). Draw symbols to represent quarter-note and eighth-note rhythms.

Rhythm: Differentiate between rhythm and beat

Pitter-Patter, Raindrops

Traditional

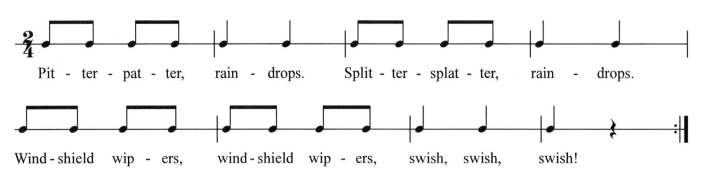

Pit - ter - pat - ter,   rain - drops.   Split - ter - splat - ter,   rain - drops.

Wind - shield wip - ers,   wind - shield wip - ers,   swish, swish,   swish!

1. Teach the chant, echoing by phrases.
2. Once the students are familiar with the chant, divide the class in half. Have one group pat the beat on the legs and the other half clap and speak the text. Switch groups.
3. Transfer the patterns to non-pitched percussion (drums for the beat, rhythm sticks for the rhythm). For further exploration, transfer the beat to bass instruments on C and G and improvise text rhythms on barred instruments (remove the F and B bars).

Jump, Jim Joe

Traditional

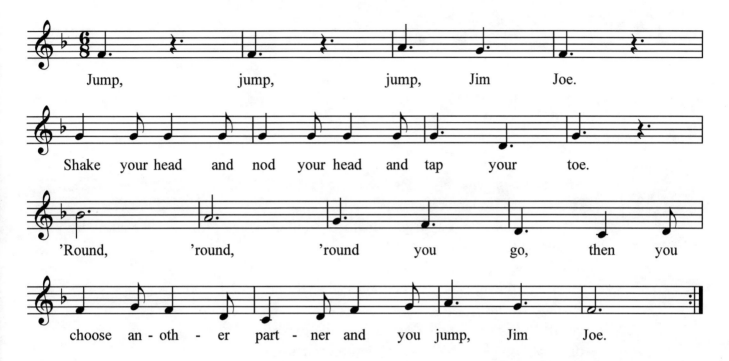

Jump, jump, jump, Jim Joe.

Shake your head and nod your head and tap your toe.

'Round, 'round, 'round you go, then you

choose an - oth – er part – ner and you jump, Jim Joe.

We now want students to think beyond phrases and realize that songs can be identified by the arrangement of their sections. The first experience with this concept is the popular folk song "Jump, Jim Joe."

1. Teach the song echoing by phrases.
2. Label the song A.
3. Place the students in groups of four. Establish each student's first, second, and third partners. This will be the order in which they choose "new" partners at the end of each time through.
4. Teach the following movement:

    Measures 1–4: Partners hold hands and jump on each word.
    Measures 5–8: Perform motions as indicated in the text.
    Measures 9–12: Partners turn in place.
    Measures 13–16: Students change partners and jump on "jump, Jim Joe."

I Like Coffee

Traditional Text
Arr. Hiller/Dupont

I   like   cof - fee,   I   like   tea;   I'd   like   you   to   fol - low   me!

Body Percussion

sol

mi

Figure 1

1. Arrange the *sol* and *mi* circles (available on the CD) to create a pitch ladder, as seen in *Figure 1*.
2. Teach the song using hand signs and then pointing to the pitches on the pitch ladder (*sol* and *mi*).
3. Display the Steady Beat Visual, and with the students, notate first the rhythm (stems only) and then the pitches (S = *sol*, M = *mi*).
4. For the B section, invite one student leader to perform the beat, using one body percussion movement (e.g., snap, clap, pat, or stamp) for the other students to perform simultaneously. Continue with new leaders.

Melody: Sing, play, and identify sol, la, *and* mi

Bounce High

Traditional

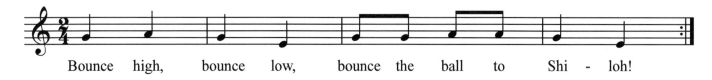

Bounce   high,   bounce   low,   bounce   the   ball   to   Shi - loh!

1. Sing the song using body levels to outline the melody; place hands on waist for the low note (*mi*), on shoulders for the middle note (*sol*), and on head for the high note (*la*).
2. Teach the following movements:
   Formation: Students in pairs.
      Measure 1: Clap own hands, then pat partner's hands high.
      Measure 2: Clap own hands, then pat own legs.
      Measures 3–4: Step, two, three, four (change places).
      Repeat.

Snail, Snail

Traditional

Snail,   snail,   snail,   snail,   creep a - round and 'round and 'round.

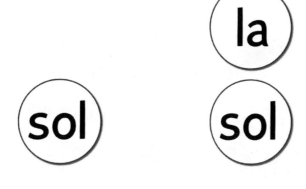

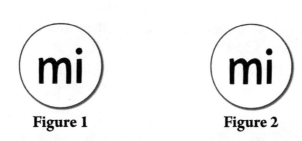

Figure 1   **Figure 2**

1. Place the *sol* and *mi* circles (available on the CD) on your board, as seen in *Figure 1* to create a pitch ladder.
2. Sing the song, pointing to the pitches. When you get to "round and," point to the empty space above *sol*. Tell the students that a pitch is missing.
3. Sing the song again using the solfège syllables, and hum on the "missing" pitch. Identify the pitch as *la*.
4. Place *la* on the pitch ladder, as seen in *Figure 2*. Teach its hand sign. Have the students sing the song with hand signs.

Bubble Bath!

Hiller/Dupont

Fill the tub with water!

Pour in the bubble bath!

Watch the bubbles grow, and grow, and grow!

Watch the bubbles pop!

Popping here, popping there, popping, popping everywhere!

Open the drain!

Watch the bubbles go down, down, down!

All gone!

The end!

1. Expressively speak the poem (unmetered) for your students.
2. In self-space, have the students create on-the-spot movements to accompany the poem.
3. Have the students sit at the barred instruments and walk them through playing the accompaniment as indicated in the table below.
4. Perform the poem with the students providing the accompaniment.

Text	Accompaniment
Bubble Bath!	Play clusters on any two pitches (2X).
Fill the tub with water!	Play clusters low to high.
Pour in the bubble bath!	Play clusters high to low.
Watch the bubbles grow, and grow, and grow!	Play *tremolos* by instrument family in additive fashion.
Watch the bubbles pop!	Make random strikes on the instruments.
Popping here, popping there, popping, popping everywhere!	Make random strikes on the instruments.
Open the drain!	Glockenspiel players strike any bars with one bar held horizontally in place of a mallet.
Watch the bubbles go down, down, down!	Play *tremolos* by instrument family in subtractive fashion.
All gone!	All play a *glissando* from high to low.
The end!	Play octave Cs.

Wind It Thisaway

Traditional

1. Draw a picture of an ice-cream cone on the board. Tell the students that it has two parts: the scoop and the cone. Have them suggest other things that have two parts (a balloon and its string, a flower and its stem, etc.). Tell them that in music, songs can also have two parts, or sections.

2. Sing the song and have the students raise their hands when you sing the new section. Teach the song. Once the class is familiar with it, label the sections A and B. Have students get in pairs and create movements for the A section and contrasting movements for the B section.

3. Play a recording of "Minuet" from *Notebook for Anna Magdalena Bach,* by Bach. Students will enjoy creating movements that show not only the form but the style of the piece as well.

One, Two, Three, Four, Five

Traditional
Arr. Hiller/Dupont

One, Two, Three, Four, Five

1. Maintain a steady beat on both legs while singing the song. Encourage your students to join you.
2. Transfer the steady beat to the bass instruments as indicated in the score.
3. Teach the woodblock and glockenspiel parts through body percussion and then transfer to the instruments.
4. Divide remaining students into two groups to perform the questions and answers as indicated.

Melody: Sing, play, and identify sol, la, *and* mi

Lucy Locket

Traditional

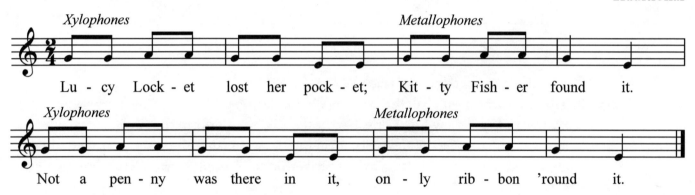

Lu - cy Lock - et lost her pock - et; Kit - ty Fish - er found it.

Not a pen - ny was there in it, on - ly rib - bon 'round it.

1. Hold up a xylophone with only the A, G, and E pitches on it. Holding it vertically shows the relationship of *la* to *sol* and *mi*.
2. Have the students sit at xylophones and metallophones with the same three pitches and play the melody as indicated on the score.

Rhythm: Notate quarter notes, two eighth notes, and quarter rests

Composing with Sticks

1. Distribute craft (Popsicle) sticks.
2. Clap four-beat rhythm patterns that include combinations of learned rhythms, and have the students notate the rhythms using the sticks on their desks or on the floor (vertical stick = quarter note, two vertical sticks with connecting stick on top = eighth notes, slanted stick = rest).

Caterpillar, Caterpillar

Hiller/Dupont

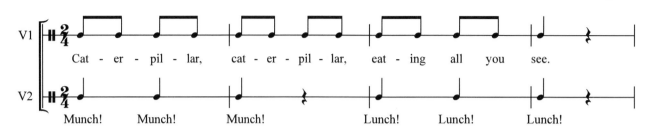

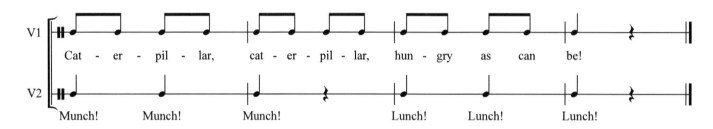

1. Teach V1. When students can perform V1, teach V2.
2. Divide class in half and perform with half the class on V1 and the other half on V2. Switch groups.
3. Read *The Very Hungry Caterpillar*, by Eric Carle, having the students perform the two-part text after the phrase "But he was still hungry" every time it occurs in the story. Enhance the story by having students play various non-pitched percussion instruments or strikes on the barred instruments to represent the various foods as they are listed.

Rain on the Green Grass

Traditional
Arr. Hiller/Dupont

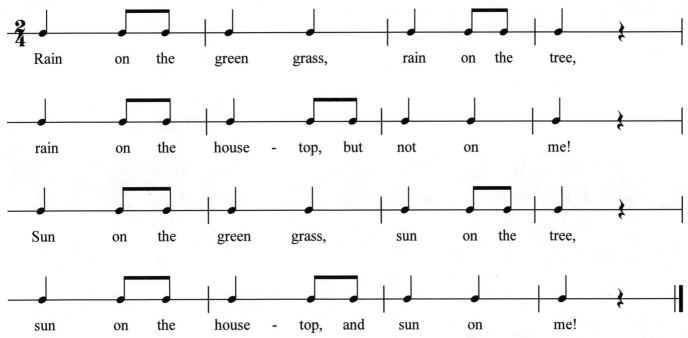

Rain on the green grass, rain on the tree,

rain on the house - top, but not on me!

Sun on the green grass, sun on the tree,

sun on the house - top, and sun on me!

1. Present the Rain on the Green Grass Chart. Teach the chant, echoing by phrases.
2. Once familiar, perform the chant while playing body percussion as indicated on the transfer chart. Repeat, internalizing the special words.
3. Next, distribute non-pitched percussion as shown on the Transfer Chart. Transfer the body percussion to non-pitched percussion. Repeat, internalizing the special words.

Transfer Chart

green grass = snap = metals

tree = clap = woods

housetop = pat = skins

not sun on me = stamp = large percussion

Sample Lesson Plan
First Grade: Rhythm

Focus: Explore combinations of quarter notes, two eighth notes, and quarter rests
Skills: Play instruments • Maintain a steady beat • Play a chord bordun

Process

1. Present the following Four-Beat Rhythm Cards:

2. Speak each rhythm card, indicating for your students to echo. Next, speak each card and have the students speak and clap. Finally, speak the cards and have the students clap the rhythms.
3. Teach the A section of "If All the World," echoing by phrases.
4. Prepare the orchestration using body percussion and then transfer the pattern to the instruments.
5. Divide the class into three groups. Teach the B section. Transfer the claps to non-pitched percussion, one family (metals, woods, skins) per group.
6. Perform the song as follows:
   Introduction: BX/BM (four measures)
   A: Song with orchestration
   B: Drink rhythm chant (first with voices, then with instruments)

Extension

As a class, create a new four-drink rhythm. List the drinks on the board and see if students can help notate the rhythm. These can also be written on cards for students to hold in front of the class when the song is performed. The B section can also be transferred to barred instruments as indicated (remove F and B bars).

If All the World

Traditional Rhyme
Arr. Hiller/Dupont

●●● **First Grade** ●●●

51

Sample Lesson Plan

First Grade: Form

Focus: AB (binary form)

Skills: Recognize A (repeated form) • Play instruments • Perform rhythmic speech • Level bordun

Run, Children, Run

Traditional
Arr. Hiller/Dupont

Process

1. Review the familiar nursery rhyme "Hickory, Dickory, Dock." Label the rhyme A. Teach the contrasting section shown below. Label this new section B. Enhance the contrast by adding movements for each section.

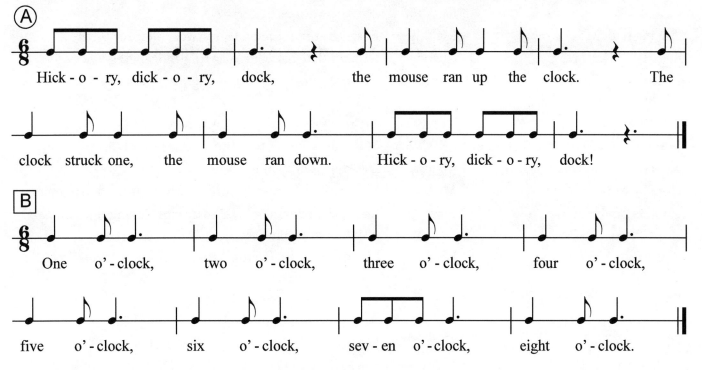

2. Teach the A section of "Run, Children, Run," echoing by phrases.
3. Prepare the orchestration with body percussion and/or text phrases and then transfer the patterns to the instruments. Assign several students to each instrument part.
4. Teach the B section, echoing by phrases. Encourage expressive speech!
5. Perform the song:
   A: Song with orchestration
   B: Speech
6. Introduce this game: With students standing in a circle, pass a beach ball to the half-note pulse (A section). On the B section, the student who has the ball at the end of the song tosses it to another child in the circle and "runs" to a barred instrument. When the class sings the song again, the student at the instrument plays E–D–C (*mi–re–do*) on "al-most day." Continue in this manner until one student remains.

Extension

Teach or review the song "Wind It Thisaway" (see page 45), echoing by phrases. Divide the class into two groups, one for the A section and one for the B section. Have each group create different movements to accompany its section. Encourage the groups to use different formations (circle, partners, alley of partners, etc.) to highlight the contrasting sections.

Kindergarten Scope and Sequence

Song/Activity	Element	Concept
I Can Walk	Rhythm	Move to various meters ($\frac{2}{4}$, $\frac{3}{4}$, $\frac{4}{4}$, $\frac{6}{8}$)
Singing with Mr. Bear	Melody	Foster in-tune singing (one, two, and three pitches)
Baa, Baa, Black Sheep	Melody	Differentiate between speaking and singing voices
Listen as I Whisper	Timbre	Explore vocal qualities (singing, speaking, whispering, and shouting)
Clap the Beat	Rhythm	Maintain a steady beat (body percussion)
Johnny Works with One Hammer	Rhythm	Maintain a steady beat (non-pitched percussion)
The Grand Old Duke of York	Melody	Develop a sense of melodic contour
Here I Come	Melody	Explore high and low (voices and non-pitched percussion)
Cobbler, Cobbler	Form	Identify phrases through chanting, singing, moving, and instrument playing
Wee Willie Winkie	Form	Identify phrases through chanting, singing, moving, and instrument playing
Engine, Engine Number Nine	Rhythm	Maintain a steady beat (speech)
Charlie Over the Ocean	Form	Perform call-and-response
Sing Your Name	Melody	Foster in-tune singing (one, two, and three pitches)
Red Light, Green Light/Walking, Walking	Rhythm	Count a silent beat
Time for Instruments	Texture	Distinguish between monophonic and polyphonic music
Hurry, Little Pony	Texture	Perform the beat while chanting and singing
This Is the Way the Ladies Ride	Timbre	Perform body percussion (snap, clap, pat, and stamp)
Rig-a-Jig-Jig	Form	Identify verse and refrain
Hickory, Dickory, Dock	Texture	Perform the beat while chanting and singing
Sing, Dance, Chant, and Play	Timbre	Identify non-pitched percussion instruments by sound and family (woods, metals, skins)
Move to the Tempo	Rhythm	Identify tempo (slow/slower; fast/faster)
Higglety, Pigglety, Pop!	Rhythm	Identify tempo (slow/slower; fast/faster)
Drip, Drip, Drip	Rhythm	Perform durations shorter and longer than the beat
Hammer Ring	Rhythm	Perform durations shorter and longer than the beat
One, Two, Tie My Shoe	Form	Learn counting songs
Hot Cross Buns	Rhythm	Perform durations shorter and longer than the beat
Bought Me a Cat	Form	Learn cumulative songs

First Grade Scope and Sequence

Song/Activity	Element	Concept
I'm Gonna Build	Rhythm	Explore quarter note, eighth note, and quarter rest through movement
Rhythm Band	Rhythm	Experience quarter note
Feel the Phrase	Form	Identify phrases in chants and songs
Eensy-Weensy Spider	Form	Identify phrases in chants and songs
Ah, vous dirais-je Maman	Form	Identify phrases in chants and songs
Little Birdie in the Tree	Form	Identify phrases that are the same and that are different
Little Bo-Peep	Texture	Perform rhythm patterns over the beat
Little Mousie	Rhythm	Identify quarter note
'Round and 'Round	Rhythm	Identify quarter rest
Bow, Wow, Wow	Melody	Listen for upward, downward, and repeated pitches
What Did You Have for Breakfast?	Melody	Sing, play, and identify *sol* and *mi*
Brown Bear, Brown Bear	Melody	Sing, play, and identify *sol* and *mi*
Drum's Birthday	Timbre	Identify and play a variety of non-pitched percussion instruments
Skip to My Lou	Form	Identify phrases that are the same and that are different
Student Rhythms	Rhythm	Experience eighth note
Seesaw	Rhythm	Identify eighth note
Pitter-Patter, Raindrops	Rhythm	Differentiate between rhythm and beat
Jump, Jim Joe	Form	Recognize A (repeated form)
I Like Coffee	Melody	Sing, play, and identify *sol* and *mi*
Bounce High	Melody	Sing, play, and identify *sol, la,* and *mi*
Snail, Snail	Melody	Sing, play, and identify *sol, la,* and *mi*
Bubble Bath!	Timbre	Explore the sound qualities of barred instruments
Wind It Thisaway	Form	Recognize AB (binary form)
Minuet	Form	Recognize AB (binary form)
One, Two, Three, Four, Five	Texture	Perform simple accompaniments on barred instruments
Lucy Locket	Melody	Sing, play, and identify *sol, la,* and *mi*
Composing with Sticks	Rhythm	Notate quarter notes, two eighth notes, and quarter rests
Caterpillar, Caterpillar	Texture	Perform simple *ostinatos* to accompany text
Rain on the Green Grass	Timbre	Transfer text rhythms to body percussion and non-pitched percussion

Instrument Glossary

SG	soprano glockenspiel		Cab.	cabasa
AG	alto glockenspiel		DR	drum
SX	soprano xylophone		SB	sandblocks
AX	alto xylophone		Tam.	tambourine
BX	bass xylophone		Tri.	triangle
SM	soprano metallophone		WB	woodblock
AM	alto metallophone			
BM	bass metallophone		Clap	clap hands
CBB	contra bass bars		Pat	pat legs
V	voice		Snap	snap fingers
SR	soprano recorder		Stamp	stamp foot

Curwen/Glover Hand Signs

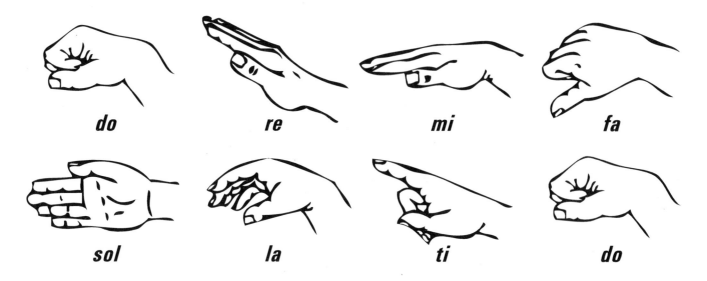

do   re   mi   fa

sol   la   ti   do

Dating back to the 18th century, these hand signs were later adopted and popularized in music education by Zoltán Kodály. The hand sign for low *do* is made near your navel. To create a physical connect to pitch, the rest of the signs are made travelling along a vertical path upward from your waist, with the hand sign for upper *do* being made at your forehead (or eye level, as some prefer). Note that the illustrations on this page show how the sign will look to you. Although shown here with the right hand, all may be made with the left or both.